Jon & Jayne's Guide to
Getting Through
School
(Mostly Intact)

Health Communications, Inc.
Deerfield Beach, Florida
www.hcibooks.com

The authors believe the information and advice presented in this book are sound and relevant. However, it is recommended that you seek the help of a certified professional if you are facing serious challenges in your life. This book is not intended as a substitute for consulting with a professional mental-healthcare practitioner.

The term "hookup" as used in this book refers to hanging out with someone you like and making your feelings known.

The pseudonym "Jon and Jayne Doe" represents a creative and qualified collective of teens and adults. All characters in this book are fictitious unless listed as one of the crew (see pages 113–117).

The Library of Congress Cataloging in Publication Data is available through the Library of Congress.

Copyright © 2009 Carol Rosenberg and Gary Rosenberg

ISBN-13: 978-0-7573-0735-5 • ISBN-10: 0-7573-0735-3

Publisher: Health Communications, Inc.
         3201 S.W. 15th Street
         Deerfield Beach, FL 33442–8190

Cover design and interior design by Carol and Gary Rosenberg

Other Issues in
The Jon & Jayne Doe Series

www.jonandjayne.com

TO Mr. B,
our favorite teacher

Jon & Jayne

PASSWORD: ⎸ ▭

This book is your password to getting
through school-related pitfalls and
predicaments, making the most of
the school year, and "surviving"
long enough to get to the next
break with a little class.

It's also the key to something different
& fun, another way to share your world.

If you forget your password,
the hint is . . . *Jon & Jayne.*

FUN

WHAT'S INSIDE...

Understand. VENT Conundrums & Solutions OH, BEHAVE! Someo story

FEATURING STORIES FROM:

- Aaron
- Allie
- Ashley
- Brittney
- Chandra
- Ellora
- Ian
- Jacob
- John
- Max
- Michael
- Ryan
- Shivani
- Skylar
- Wheeler

Hey! Welcome to Issue #3! If you don't already know us from Issues #1 and #2, we're Jon Doe & Jayne Doe (no relation, just good friends). We represent people **like you** who want to be heard **LOUD & CLEAR.**

In Issue #1, we made some new friends and "got" the **guy** or **girl** to notice us (hopefully). Then, in Issue #2, we threw an **awesome** party (or went to one)—and everybody got home all in **one piece.** Whew! Now it's time to **talk** about that thing that seems to take up most of our time. **School! Ahhhhhhhhhhhhhhhh.** It's not that bad. Really. In fact, you might even think school is **cool.** (Well, at least it's got all the letters for "cool.")

---

*Welcome to **O**ur **W**orld

They (whoever *they* are) came up with the idea of school to prepare us for the **future** (a big ol' "F"), but it's the **present** we gotta get through to get there. School can be fun, **scary**, exciting, boring, hard, **easy**—you name it. School can be just about anything to **different** people. And different parts of it can make us feel a bunch of different ways. **What's it to you?**

Lots of people had **lots** to say for this issue. And, of course, we've got our own stuff to say. Whatever. We just **hope** this issue **helps** all of us make it through our school "daze" academically, socially, and physically. So, **let's do it**. . . .

The "7F World"

We live in a world of **7Fs**—friends, fun, fights, family, feelings, fashion, and flirting. It's probably a lot like your world. We have **concerns** about the future (another "F"!) and about getting by in school (no "F" for that) and in social **situations**. It's not always easy, and sometimes it's really **tough**. But we all seem to get **thru it** somehow.

We want to know what you—and people like you—have to say. Sharing our **feelings** on different subjects can help us make sense of this **7F world**.

Be Heard. Be Yourself.

cHaT_

JD GaTEr 110:   hey jayne how come u werent at practice

JaynE SaYs 611: youd never believe me if I told you

JD GaTEr 110:   tell me

JaynE SaYs 611: i had detention

JD GaTEr 110:   what u? no way

JaynE SaYs 611: it happens to the best of us

JD GaTEr 110:   whadya do

JaynE SaYs 611: I forgot to turn off my phone before english. ms G was in the middle of reading a poem when it went off. she sent me to the principal

JD GaTEr 110:   they wouldnt give you a break, just this once

JaynE SaYs 611: zero tolerance and u know how seriously ms G takes her poetry readings

JD GaTEr 110: well that'll teach ya. who was calling btw

JaynE SaYs 611: it was a wrong number

JD GaTEr 110: LOL.... what r u doing now

JaynE SaYs 611: studying for the math test

JD GaTEr 110: me too... wanna come over and study together

JaynE SaYs 611: I laugh too much when we get together... I'll end up failing

JD GaTEr 110: u r right we don't make good study partners. we're better at other things

JaynE SaYs 611: oh, like what?

JD GaTEr 110: have fun studying

JaynE SaYs 611: jon!

JD GaTEr 110: what

JaynE SaYs 611: oh forget it. see u at school

JD GaTEr 110: nite

JaynE SaYs 611: g'nite

What's your story?

THE SCENARIOS

Where do you fit in?

School is back! The last break was a blast, but another round of school days is here. Schedules, homework, teachers, activities, tests, sports, friends, projects, long lunch lines, and so on. Wondering how you're gonna get through it all . . . again? Don't worry, we've got some advice for you.

Right in the thick of things? Maybe it's not going how you planned. You're hoping there's time to salvage the situation before summer. There's usually time to save something, no matter how bleak things look.

Grades up, friends down? So you're not having a problem keeping up with all the work, but the social scene isn't playing out for you. You're looking to make some friends. School's a great place for that!

Too much on your calendar? Maybe you're so busy spending time with your friends or always at practice, and you "forgot" that schoolwork's gotta

get done if you want the grades. You want to figure out how to fit it all in. You just need to balance your interests.

Teacher's fave . . . NOT? Maybe there's one teacher in particular you just can't seem to get along with. Or maybe you don't know how to relate to your teachers at all. You just need to figure out how to connect.

Always studying, barely passing? Sometimes no matter how much you go over things, you just can't seem to "get" it. For some of us, it's tough to keep up with everything that school throws at us. Hope we can help!

Got bully? That's a problem lots of us have faced one way or another in school. No matter how many friends you have or how "cool" you are, sometimes somebody decides you are the one to pick on. Hey, it happens, but you can learn to deal with it.

Looking for an after-school activity? You want to get involved, but don't know which activity or activities fit your personality and talents best. Figuring it out just takes some thought and planning.

Just curious? OK, so you just want to read a good book and get to know what we're all about. You want to know what people like you are thinking on stuff that concerns us all—some of it's important, some is trivial, but it all matters one way or another.

■ ■ ■ ■ ■

In this **issue**, you'll find 5 keywords. You'll need these to unlock the **clues** to the **Drama**.

How will you know when you find a keyword? **Easy**. We'll say something like, "So, that's the keyword." Couldn't be much easier than that!

When you find a keyword, go to jonandjayne.com, click on "OH, THE DRAMA" and follow the directions. Each keyword unlocks a clue. Solve the drama in as few clues as possible.

GOOD LUCK!

AHHHH!
No iNTERNET?!
SEE PAGE 110.

Oh, the Drama!

There's a bully who's been picking on Brett, a smart kid at our school. Ray, the bully (who happens to be one of the jocks), heard Brett talking crap to a teacher's aide at lunchtime about how jocks are all muscle with very little brainpower and that school should be just for academics. We know that's not true, but Brett doesn't deserve getting his books knocked off his desk or his lunch sprayed with cologne for just saying what was on his mind.

So, after a few days of bullying, the coach got wind of what was going on, and all the team members had to watch a bunch of movies with bullies in them, and write a paper about why bullying is wrong. Ray ended up learning a lesson, and he even wrote an excellent paper on his favorite "bully" movie. See if you can figure out which movie turned out to be his favorite.

Learning

LOG ON
TO OUR WEBSITE,
WWW.JONANDJAYNE.COM,
AND JOIN THE 7F COMMUNITY.
POST CONUNDRUMS, SHARE STORIES,
TELL THE WORLD, TAKE THE SURVEYS,
GET ANSWERS TO THE QUICKIES,
SOLVE THE DRAMA, AND MORE.
SEE U THERE AND
IN HERE!

We've Got CLASS!

Whether it's the **first** day (with no end in sight) or day **111**, we've got lots of stuff in our appointment books (even if we don't actually have appointment books) like getting up on time, being **"prepared"** in more ways than one, going to classes, dealing with teachers, eating lunch, socializing with **friends**, dodging **bullies**, participating in activities during and after school, doing **homework**, studying for **exams**, getting projects done, updating **curious** parents, and . . . **Wow**, like isn't that enough? How do we get it all done, in just a **day**?!

Sometimes we might fall **behind** in one area or subject, sometimes in a few, and **sometimes** in all of them. Or maybe not. Either way, how do we deal with all the **pressure**, come out ahead, and have **FUN** at the same time?

That's a tough question, but we've got a really good answer: **balance**. That's the keyword. When we balance schoolwork, activities, and socializing, we've pretty much got it made. It's finding that balance that can be **tough**.

It's virtually impossible to be the best in everything all the time.

We hope that what we've got to say in this issue (and what our **friends** have to say) can help you find your own sense of **balance**. We've tried to cover it all (or at least a lot of it, cause it's really **hard** to cover **everything**, you know).

So, read on to **discover** how people like us get through the school year and make it all the way to summer **break** once again. Tell us what works for you when you get a chance at the 7F Forum. What you know could **help** someone else.

"I think the thing to do is to enjoy the ride while you're on it."

—Johnny Depp

The X Factor

When we **really** thought about it and **brainstormed** with our friends, we realized that the best **classes** all have one important thing in common. It doesn't matter what the **subject** is, it doesn't even matter if it was your favorite or least **favorite** subject the year before . . . we think what makes a class good **depends** on this one very important thing: the . . .

TEACHER

A GOOD TEACHER	A LAME TEACHER
has a good sense of humor	doesn't even crack a smile
explains things clearly	is just confusing
gives good notes	depends too much on textbooks

cont'd

13

A GOOD TEACHER	A LAME TEACHER
is interested in what we have to say	doesn't listen to us
doesn't give tons of homework	gives way too much homework
makes up fair exams and helps us prepare	is tougher than he or she needs to be
offers extra help	is never available
did we say "has a good sense of humor"?	has no personality
is enthusiastic	yells a lot
treats us like people, not kids	always talks down to us

Sure, the teacher's a **major factor**, but what else makes a class a good one? Classes where we have some **good friends** make sitting through the period a bit more fun (or at least we have someone to **complain** with later). Of course how well we do in a particular subject also plays a big role in what we might call our **best** class.

When you've got it all—a good **subject**, a good **teacher**, and some good **friends** to sit next to, you've got it made. It can't always be like that, so if you're totally out of **luck**, the only thing you can do is **try** your hardest and don't give up!

SYNC WITH YOUR TEACHERS

Teachers don't disappear when the bell rings. They're actual people who exist outside school. Like us, they have up days, down days, habits, talents, hobbies, strengths, weaknesses, and challenges. So the first step in getting in sync is realizing that your teachers are just people doing what they need (and hopefully want) to do to get by in the world—and not all of them can be fun, fascinating, and friendly. You've gotta make who you get work for you.

● **Get to class before the bell rings with the right stuff.** Get your homework and projects done on time. If you're late a lot, your teacher will probably assume you don't care about the class. Not good.

● **Be nice to your teacher.** You don't have to get all overly friendly, but at least say hi to him or her when you get to class. It always helps to make eye contact—without that, there's no real connection.

● **Don't talk your teacher's ear off.** Keep in mind that you're just one student among a bunch of others. Say what you have to say, but keep it short and "sweet."

● **Take an interest in your teacher's subject.** Even if you think it's boring, you might find it more interesting if you can figure out how it applies to your life or your future. Any knowledge you get now may come in handy someday (even if it's just for next week's test).

● **Ask questions, but don't go overboard.** Questioning (aka challenging) everything your teachers say will probably annoy them. Ask questions when you want more information or need clarification.

● **Teachers like it when you are up front with them.** If you're having trouble in a class, schedule some time to talk to your teacher during his or her free period. Be honest about the problem—your teacher will probably be willing to help.

● **If you and your teacher just don't get along, speak to your guidance counselor.** He or she can act as a go-between to help you build a better relationship. Or ask your parents for help.

Meet Mr. B, The Cool English Teacher

I n this issue, we got the **coolest** teacher we could find to give us all some advice. Since our friend **Skylar** introduced us to him, we asked her if she would make the official intro to you. Here's what she had to say about **Mr. B:**

Freshman year was a drag. Once I got to high school, the work got harder, the teachers got meaner, and the upper classmen "exercised their authority." I didn't have any "slack off" classes. Every class was hard. But there was one class (the last class of the day) where I would be able to have fun (and still learn). That class was Mr. B's English class.

It wasn't an easy class, but it was the best because of him. He was one of a kind... the best teacher I've ever had, and let me tell you, he's going to be a hard teacher to

top. It wasn't only his great personality
that kept the class entertaining, but also
the activities he planned for us. We used to
do things, from acting out Romeo and Juliet
to shooting plastic animals into a box, as
part of a review. He kept us interested,
which made us want to learn from him.

He always treated us like we were people,
not students or little kids. He talked to us
about things that mattered and understood
what we were going through at such a hard
age. I learned so much from him because
he is such an awesome role model. He's got
some good advice for all of us. So listen up.

−Skylar H.

Thanks, Skylar!
Check out Mr. B's advice
on socializing (page 30) and
Mr. B's advice on academics
(page 41).

That's him.
−Jon

He's sooo Cute!
−Jayne

You got a crush
on him, Jayne?

Nah, Jon, just
admiring his looks.

Allie's story

Math Made "Easy"

Ah . . . math, one of my least favorite subjects. But that all changed when I met Mr. D. I liked him right away. For a teacher, he looks young, and he is smart, has a great sense of humor, and a friendly personality. That's why so many kids like him. He acts more like a friend than a teacher, and that's why he is my favorite. (Of course, he is also an amazing math teacher.) Although he treats us like his friends, we all treat him with respect, and he doesn't take nonsense from anyone. He's available before school or after school for extra help. He's good at breaking down problems and putting them into steps so the work is easier to understand.

Mr. D wants all his students to do well. Before tests, there is a complete study guide so what's on the test comes as no surprise. He also gives us lots of opportunities to bring up our grades. We can take a test home and correct our mistakes for an extra four points. This doesn't mean the class was easy—it wasn't easy at all. Mr. D just made it less hard.

Mr. D is always surrounded by students . . . between classes, before school, after school, in the hallways. People are just drawn to him. I don't have him this year, but I still visit him on my way to my classes, and I stop in after school to say bye. He always has a minute for everybody, whether you are in his class or not. I hope I have him next year.

—Allie M.

Teachers like Mr. D—no matter what subject they teach—make getting up on school days a little easier. Why can't all teachers be like that?*

If you don't have a teacher like Allie's, try to find something positive about the teachers you do have, even if it's a real stretch.

*Cause they have to be themselves.

Wheeler's

story

Teachers?

I think it's safe to say that we all have teachers we like . . . and some we don't like. Or at least, most of us do. Some teachers you might buy an apple for, even if that's just downright weird, and some teachers you may be secretly "plotting against" because you know they're secretly "plotting against" you. Sometimes you have a good teacher, but they teach a bad or boring subject. Maybe you're just the kind of person who resents all authority and will never have a favorite teacher. That's fine, because we can choose to like or dislike anyone we want to.

Who your favorite teachers are depend on things like what subjects you like and what type of personality you have. But if you are the type of person who likes to classify your teachers, then here's how I usually look at it:

Good teachers need to have certain personality traits. They need to have a good sense of humor and be able to dish out "school appropriate" jokes. Also, they need to have a perfect limit on the talking level in their classes. I mean, if you stick a bunch of teenagers in a place that they generally (I said generally) don't like, of course we'll talk and socialize with each other. But they can't let things get to out of control because then they can't teach, and they're no longer a "good" teacher. Another trait (which really isn't a trait) is what subject they teach. There are definitely a few teachers I'm prejudiced against just because they teach something I don't like. After all, they chose to teach that subject.

—Wheeler B.

Wheeler's right on a lot of accounts. A good sense of humor is one of the best traits a teacher can have. What's that? Wheeler's not done? Oh, sorry, there's more . . .

More from Wheeler

I want to tell you a funny story about my science teacher. After winter break, we found two iguanas that died during one of the cold fronts. My science teacher preserved them for a dissection. She picked a few volunteers—and I was one of the lucky ones.

Don't worry, for those of you who are a little on the squeamish side, I won't go into detail about the dissection, but it was pretty interesting—we learned a lot. The next day, my teacher brought the stitched-up iguana into class . . . as a puppet! Some of the kids thought it was disgusting. But I thought it was one of the funniest things that ever happened at school.

Gross, Wheeler! We know people who have iguanas as pets. They are sooo not gonna like that part of your story. Yeah, it's true that the iguanas were already dead—but yuck! We guess it was a learning experience, but puppets?! Really.

This just goes to show you that teachers sometimes do pretty wacky things. For more crazy things teachers have done, read on. . . .

YOUR TEACHER DID WHAT?

TO EXPLAIN THE THEORY OF GRAVITY, MY SCIENCE
TEACHER THREW A SHOE AT ME AND HIT ME IN THE HEAD.
HE DIDN'T MEAN TO HIT ME, AND EVEN THOUGH IT HURT,
IT WAS PRETTY FUNNY AND EVERYONE LAUGHED.

DURING THE ANNUAL STANDARDIZED TESTS, ONE OF THE
PROCTORS FELL ASLEEP DURING THE EXAM. SOMEONE
SNAPPED A PIC OF HIM WITH A CELL PHONE. (WE DIDN'T
TELL ON HIM, BUT WE'VE GOT THE EVIDENCE JUST
IN CASE WE NEED IT.)

ONE DAY, MY TEACHER DRESSED UP AS A BIKER AND
SHOUTED THROUGH A MEGAPHONE AT ALL THE GIRLS TO
TAKE OFF THEIR MAKEUP. WHAT WAS THAT ALL ABOUT?

MY TEACHER BAKED COOKIES WITH A SPECIAL INGREDIENT:
EARTHWORMS. WE WEREN'T FORCED TO EAT THEM, BUT I
WAS BRAVE AND TRIED ONE. IT TASTED LIKE BACON.

OUR GEOGRAPHY TEACHER WAS SO OBLIVIOUS THAT HE
DIDN'T REALIZE SOMEONE HAD TAPED THE ANSWERS
TO THE TEST WE WERE TAKING ONTO HIS BACK.

MY MATH TEACHER IS OBSESSED WITH MAKING THE
"SHHH" SOUND. ONE WEEK, MY FRIEND KEPT A TALLY
OF JUST HOW MANY TIMES HE SAID IT: ALMOST 2,000.

MY TEACHER "MADE" ME EAT ALLIGATOR. IT TASTED
LIKE CHICKEN.*

* Doesn't everything?

R y a n ' s

s
t
o
r
y

Weird Science

My advanced science teacher is weird. He
drives a Harley to school in a leather jacket (even
though it's really hot where we live). He trades in
the leather for a white lab coat when we do labs.
He shouts out random stuff during class, which
makes us laugh, and sometimes throws erasers
when he's angry (which is rare). We've gotten
pretty good at dodging them.

In another school, he set the ceiling of his class-
room on fire. He was doing an experiment to show
the violent reaction between pure sodium and
water, but he'd forgotten to empty the beaker
from the previous experiment. When he added

the sodium, the beaker exploded onto the ceiling. You'd think he'd learn from his mistake, but he did it again in our school. This time the beaker exploded into a camera that was magnifying the experiment. (Bet that came out of his paycheck!)

Once he dressed up as Albert Einstein to teach us about atoms. He wore a wig and mustache and spoke with a German accent. He called himself Albert "Two"stein, since "ein" means "one" in German and he was the second. That was just weird, but he drew a big crowd of teachers—and the principal. And I actually learned a thing or two.

This guy is a cool teacher because he makes his class (and learning) fun. He's a little weird and crazy, but to me, that's what science is all about.

—Ryan "Chili" P.

Science is strange if you think about it. A lot of it seems like magic: invisible fields, puffs of smoke, explosions, things existing in two places at once. . . . Sometimes it's hard to wrap your head around it. That's why it's so important to have a science teacher who makes learning this stuff interesting. It's a major bonus if he or she can also make it fun.

LET'S EAT

When we polled our friends and our friends' friends, **99.9999%** of them said lunch is their favorite subject. **Hmmmm.** Is lunch even a subject? Guess it could be, but what are we studying? When you really think about it, that's an easy **question** to answer . . . each other.

Who's **hanging** with who? Who's **wearing** what? Who's alone? Who's sitting at *that* table? Who's **fighting**? Who's **flirting**? And just what the heck is that gray lump on the **lunch** tray—really?

Lunch is when we can blow off some **steam**, make some **connections**, make some **plans**, oh, and eat some **food**. (Let's not forget that!)

Lunch is also when the **cliques** come together. Sounds **stereotypical**, yeah, but there's no doubt that when lunch **launches**, the cliques **clump**. Victoria says:

"Cliques are a reality. You have the basketball girls and guys at adjoining tables, and the preps hanging with the football players, the geeks with the geeks, the emos crying with the emos, and so on. I don't think there's anything wrong with it. It's just the way things are. People hang out with the people they have things in common with. I know I hang out with the people who are most like me because they make me feel like I belong."

Not everyone feels like Victoria does and not everyone has the same **experience** at school. Lunch is also when the loners seem most **alone**. This is what Austin said about that:

"I'm not really into hanging out with other people. At lunch, it's not so much that I want to be with other people. I like being by myself. But when other people see me alone, I get a little embarrassed, like they're all thinking, *What's wrong with him? Why doesn't he have any friends?* Truth is, I'm just not social."

We all know people like Victoria and Austin—but there are also **people** in between. That's where a lot of us fall. Either way, **socializing** *is* a big part of lunch, and that's why it's the keyword here.

Another big part of lunch is, of course, the whole "eating thing." Some people **buy** it, some **bring** it, and some **skip** it. The last choice isn't such a great idea. We need to eat to get through the day with at least a little **brainpower** left over. Chugging soda isn't gonna do it for very long.

So, what's the food like at your school? Tasty? Nasty? Do they have **healthy** choices? Do they use **styrofoam** lunch trays? (*Not* biodegradable.) If you're not **happy** with what's on the menu—or what it's served on—speak up, start a **petition**, and make a **difference**! At the very least, bring something from home if you'd rather **pass** on the school's version of **food**.

WHAT'S IN IT?!

Wheeler B. takes a close look at his lunch tray before eating (if he actually ends up eating). This is just some of what he's come across in his food:

- hair (haven't we all, but yuck) • spiders (that's a new one) • bug eggs (OMG!) • cockroaches (can anything be grosser? yeah, bug eggs) • stickers (very strange!) • fungus (on the grape juice)

That's nasty. What's the grossest thing you've seen in school food? Tell us at jonandjayne.com. But pleeeze, don't make us gag—we gotta eat too.

CLIQUE OUTSIDE THE LUNCH BOX

A few pages back, Victoria said **cliques** are just the way it is—people hang out with people who are most like them cause it makes them feel like they **belong**. Sure, we all want to feel like we belong. But whether or not we're in with the "**cool**" crowd (or in a crowd at all), we've gotta remember that we all **belong**—even if it's just to the same school.

Lunch is a good time to try expanding your social **network**—you may discover that the kid in the corner is full of **fascinating** info, that the girl with acne is beautiful **inside**, that the jock has more on his mind than football, or that the **stuck-up** "biatch" has a **sensitive** side. Talk to different people whenever you get the **chance**—you'll learn more about the world and the people in it . . . and maybe even get to **know yourself** a little better.

It's true—**socializing** is easier for some than for others. No matter who you are, you're sure to be **judged**, and **rejection** is always a possibility when you put yourself out there. But that doesn't mean it's not worth the **effort**.

ON SOCIALIZING

66 You can't please everyone. If you change your style a little bit just to please Natalie, then Susan will stop talking to you, Jake will never sit at your lunch table again, Ganelle might hang around more often, but then so would her best friend, who's more annoying than a fresh cold sore. No matter what you do, you'll have some people accepting your decisions about your hair, clothes, friends, activities, etcetera, and still other people condemning it. The mixed and ever-changing results are stressful enough to give you even more acne than you already have.

It's hard enough to decide what you like about life and about yourself, let alone trying to cater to what all your friends like, or worse yet, what people you don't even know like. Respect yourself and give yourself the decency of doing what you feel is most comfortable for you.

Whoever can't respect that will eventually learn the truth the hard way; when it's too late to do something about it and they suffer from their own, self-induced humiliation.

If you like wearing jeans and a white T-shirt, wear it. If you really enjoy chess, join the club. If you really hate going to concerts, don't go. If you're not in the mood for a good-night kiss, turn your cheek. Remember that the only one who will have to live with your decisions is you. **"**

Mr. B pretty much said what we've been saying since Issue #1: **Be yourself!** It's tough to do that, of course, when we're so busy worrying about what everyone else is going to think or say behind our back or right to our face.

That's where **courage** comes in. Knowing that you are going to be judged no matter what you do and doing it anyway because it feels right for you takes a lot of guts—and may just make you stronger in the long run. Hey, it really is worth taking a chance.

Judgment—the keyword here—is a fact of life and it's not gonna go away. It's how you deal with it that can really make a difference.

Ashley's story

Clique Anywhere

So we all know what it means to be in a clique, right? I mean, there are preps, there are rich kids, there are jocks, and then there are the emo kids, the drama geeks, and the nerds. At school it's really obvious that a lot of people belong to one clique and socialize with only that group of people. I, on the other hand, tend to "clique anywhere."

I have friends from not one, not two, but from every clique. I have friends who shop at the trendiest clothing stores, and I have other friends who shop at alternative stores. Some of my friends go to the movies a lot or work backstage at the shows, while others just play sports or study for hours.

It's pretty cool having friends from every clique because you learn a lot more about everything and become really well rounded. Plus you get to experience lots of new things and meet really cool people. It can be kind of hard, though, because if you want to hang out with a bunch of friends from different cliques (like at lunch), they typically won't get along or relate to each other. It's too bad.

I find it really easy to talk to anyone because I can relate to everyone in some way. I look past the stereotypes and actually see what I have in common with people I meet. That's the way to do it. Take it from me, the girl who's always crossing cliques, you'll leave school with everyone knowing your name and you'll feel really great.

—*Ashley B.*

Ashley makes it sound so easy (and maybe for her it is), but we know it's tough for some people to be "friends" with everyone. Start small with a few good friends and grow from there. When it comes to friends, we say quality before quantity. And remember, there's a difference between friends and acquaintances—we talked about that in Issue #1. Missed it? Check it out!

Shivani's story

Don't "Brand" Me!

I always used to go to school without ever thinking twice about what I was wearing. I never used to think about which brand I was wearing or which company my clothes were from. I thought that I should wear what I was comfortable in and not what people around me were wearing. But then I went to middle school. And I saw that 99.9% of the people were wearing popular brands. That night I went home and searched up and down in my closet, knowing for sure that I had some clothes with those labels. But no. I couldn't find a single shirt or bottom in that closet with those names.

The next day I decided that I needed some clothes that were "in." So my mom and I went to one of the trendy stores, and I almost had a heart attack. $25 for a tank top that you could buy anywhere else in the world for $3. My mom and I walked right out the door when we saw how expensive everything was. We stopped at the next trendy store. When we saw that most of the stuff in that store was more reasonably priced than in the first, we bought a few things.

I got home late that night and all I wanted to do was sink into my bed. I laid out my new clothes on my chair. I stared at them, pleased with the day and knowing that I finally had some clothes that were "in." I couldn't wait till Monday so I could wear something new.

Soon Monday came and passed like any other day. After that, I mixed and matched my new clothes with my older clothes. One day I realized that I wasn't even aware if I was wearing my "trendy" clothes or my old clothes because they all came down to just being clothes. I realized then that symbols can't define whether or not your clothes are cool. They have to feel fun and be comfy to wear.

From then on, I didn't care whether or not my clothes were a particular brand that everyone else was wearing. I looked for clothes that described my personality and who I really am.

—Shivani P.

Clothes . . . they can tell people a lot about our personalities, or they can disguise who we really are inside, or they can have no meaning at all. What we choose to wear one day can reflect our mood, what we have planned, what was clean, or what the dress code is. Some clothes are status symbols, social statements, stylistic preferences, or just what's affordable. If you're into "trendy," remember it doesn't have to have an expensive label to be stylish.

While you're at it, why not set your own trend? A popular girl we know wore bowling shoes to school, expecting to start a new trend. She got laughed at, but it was gutsy.

What you wear doesn't make you who you are, but what you choose to wear becomes part of you—at least for the day. So put on something that makes you comfortable in your outer skin. Dress to impress . . . yourself.

Making the Grade

not everyone can be an **"A"** student. Not everyone can be a **"B"** student, even. Some people can ace some subjects but not all of them. Take **Albert Einstein**, for instance. He excelled at physics and science (**duh**), but he had trouble in other subjects (like French). Bet there are lots of people out there who have a similar **problem**.

Do you know a kid or two who barely pays **attention** in class and still gets **A**'s? Is that you? Chances are if you're reading this part with great interest, you're not that kid. And you know what? That's **okay.** Lots of people who aren't in line for valedictorian go on to achieve **xtraordinary** things in their lifetimes. It really doesn't matter how **"book smart"** someone is, what matters is how smart they are about what they do with the smarts they've got. **Common sense** goes a long way. Got some?

OK, so you're not the **smartest** in class. There's only one thing you can do, and you already know what that is: your **best**. Yeah, yeah, you've heard it all before. We all have. But you know what? It works. You just gotta **figure** out what your best is and then do it. Have you given up trying to **understand** something because you've had trouble grasping it? Have you given up **studying** for tests because you do poorly anyway? There's help out there if you know where to look.

Start with your **teacher**. Be honest about the difficulty you're having (he or she probably already knows). Try to **identify** what's causing your problems. Your teacher can set you up with a **tutor** or with extra help. Nothing's wrong with that. If you get your **parents** involved, you can sign up for a learning center. Yeah, making the grade might be a drag, but if you can do better, you'll feel **better**!

Check out my no-fail study tips on the next page.

Um, Jayne, nobody likes reading test-taking tips.

Jon, duh. It's a book about school—it couldn't be avoided!

JAYNE'S NO-FAIL STUDY TIPS

1 Studying begins in class, even before an exam is scheduled. So, try to avoid daydreaming while your teacher is talking. In other words, listen, even if you don't think it's interesting. It's no secret that he or she is going to say something you'll need to know.

2 Take good notes! Good notes are ones you can read later 'cause you wrote them neat enough so that they don't look like frantic scribbles the next time you look at 'em. You don't have to write down every word you hear, but definitely write down key terms and other info your teacher says is important.

3 Review your notes later, and if you don't get something, ask your teacher for clarification. Don't wait till you have a whole bunch of incomprehensible notes before you start asking questions.

4 Actually read the textbook pages that your teacher assigns. Sometimes it helps to read out loud to yourself. You can make this fun by reading with a fake accent or even by singing the words. Sounds crazy, but try it—it might make a difference.

5 Go to extra help if it's offered, or get a tutor if something's really confusing you.

6 Study groups are great, but if you get together with friends to study and you eat chips, chat, and chug chocolate milk instead, it's not gonna help. Make sure your study partners are serious if you're serious about passing your test. (That's why I don't study w/Jon.)

7 As soon as you hear about an upcoming test, figure out how many days you have to study for it. Everyone needs a different amount of time to really absorb the info. Set aside some time every day to review the material that's supposed to be on the test.

8 Read your notes out loud to yourself and use a highlighter to highlight really important stuff. Rewrite the notes and ask yourself questions to see if you can answer them correctly. Use mnemonics to remember key terms. Don't know what mnemonics is? Google it.

9 Record your notes into a voice recorder and play it back while you're doing something else, like falling asleep or exercising. It just might sink in.

10 Don't stress out on the day of the test—you might forget important stuff that you know.

If you've followed these tips, be confident that you have taken all the necessary steps to do well.

These tips really work for me. I don't ace every test, but I do pretty well overall.

ON ACADEMICS

66 Academia is just one path among thousands in the maze of life. The most important part of surviving the academic journey is maintaining some sort of organization. An assignment notebook—a calendar where you can write down all your duties and deadlines—will work as a road map that will keep you from getting lost, from getting swallowed up by the stresses of school. If you get into the habit of writing in this calendar after every class, even to remind yourself that you have no homework for the evening, you'll know exactly where you're going. **In these jungles, you don't want any surprises.**

Tests, assignments, and homework can seem overwhelming when you don't have any organization or preparation. A big project, for example, is like a cryptozoological creature. (Do you know what that is? If not, you need to study more. Grab a dictionary!) These tasks, these creatures, are things you've never seen before, something you never knew existed. You need to identify what this **strange, freaky animal** is before you can do anything about it. Can you befriend it and ride on its back for the rest of the journey? **Should you kill it and eat it?** If this strange animal is called a *Researchus paperius,* you might ask yourself how long it is, how much it weighs, what it eats to stay alive. Read the directions, over and over again if you need to, until you understand clearly what is required of you. Only once you clearly understand what the assignment is can you conquer it.

Don't forget, too, that **mind has more power than matter** in this world. If you trust and believe that you can do well on a ten-point project or a six hundred-point presentation, you can. If you tell yourself that you can't, you won't. These animals can read your mind!

This is your future, whether you want to admit that right now or not. Talk to older students who already know better (and don't forget that teachers and parents were once students too and might know a thing or two as well). **Work hard now, party harder later.** If you choose to play now, you'll be lost in those jungles, cut up, and bleeding from thorns, bug bites, and paper cuts. Don't let the dinosaurs or dioramas swallow you up alive! 99

Thanks, Mr. B!

Jacob's story

Easing Into the Essay

We all know the biggest part of school is homework. And, well, we also know that the hardest homework assignments are essays. But if you know what to do, they're not hard. And I'm here to tell you what to do!

Pick a topic that interests you. This will help you in several ways. I always remember information better if I have even a remote interest in learning it, so it means less flipping through notes later on. Also, you won't get bored as easily and will probably end up working for longer than you normally would. This also helps to give you a feeling that you got some personal gain out of the effort, which is something notably absent from most schoolwork.

My freshman year, I had to write a paper on a poet for my English class. I was assigned a poet who didn't interest me at all. While doing my research, I came across another poet who I thought was very interesting. I asked my teacher if I could make the switch. Once she said okay, I found that everything was a lot easier for me to do. The actual paper, for example, took me about half the time to write as it took other people, and it was twice as long as some of the other papers.

Just as important is staying organized. Get your hands on a one-inch binder with three rings— that's your best bet. You can usually print out all the information you need, or photocopy it if it's from a book. This way, all your reference material can be easily kept in the same spot. You can even hole-punch index cards, if that's what you take your notes on.

For me, I've found that the best way of staying organized with my notes is to write an outline for the paper, and then label the notecards by which part of the outline that they belong in. This way, once you sort the index cards according to the outline, you never have to go hunting through your notes to find the next point you want to write about, because it'll be on top of your stack of cards.

These tips should help you to save time on some of the most major parts of school, and maybe even make it easier for you.

—Jacob C.

Writing comes naturally to some people—like us. For others, it's not so easy. Next time you are faced with writing a paper, do all your research first, then try talking to a friend about what you want to say. Hearing yourself actually speak it will make it easier to write it down. Using a voice recorder to help you remember what you said is also a good idea.

Sometimes the hardest part is just getting started. If you're having real trouble, write down whatever comes to mind on the topic, even if it doesn't make perfect sense. In other words, brainstorm on paper—you don't have to use complete sentences. Once you get it all down, you can make sense of it later. That'll be easier to do if you enter it into a Word doc.

NOT TOP SECRET
BRETT SMART

Brett is probably one of the smartest students at our school. He aces every test and gets along with all his teachers. He manages to avoid all sorts of academic chaos. We asked him how come it's so easy for him, and this is what he said:

School means a lot to me, probably because that's where I excel. While other kids are out socializing or playing sports, I'm home studying or working on special projects. I like to learn—that's just who I am. Someday I'll use what I learn to make the world a better place, sort of like Bill Gates did. Everyone calls me a "brainiac," but I don't think I'm a genius or anything. I need to work really hard to keep getting high grades.

Being called a "brain" or a "nerd" bothers me. And sometimes I just want to be like everyone else and not care as much about school. But that's not who I am. I guess I'm smart for a reason—the way other people are athletic or musically inclined. It's my talent, and I'm smart enough to know I've got to be myself—no matter how difficult it is sometimes.

A not-so-good student . . .

- teases or bullies other kids
- has a bad attitude toward learning
- creates a ruckus whenever there's a chance
- is always late with assignments and projects
- falls asleep or zones out during lectures
- doesn't contribute to the discussion
- texts, listens to music, or plays games during classes

LOTS of us fall somewhere in the middle!

a good student . . .

- studies for tests and quizzes
- gets assignments completed on time
- brings the right books and materials to class
- spends some time on extracurricular activities
- doesn't get all stressed out over getting something wrong
- is friendly to teachers and classmates
- listens and participates during classes

eNLIGHTeNMeNt

"The beginning of knowledge is the discovery
of something we do not understand."

—Frank Herbert (a guy with lots of imagination
and the author of the Dune sci-fi series)

Understand.

Understand.

Knowledge is power!

There's so much **information** coming at us from all **different** directions and all different places that we can't possibly **absorb** it all, but we need to find a way to pick and choose what's **important** enough to hold on to. We've got to understand this information, and if we don't, we need to ask **questions**.

Knowledge is simply putting what we've learned to use in the **real world**. Sure there's stuff we have to memorize for tests, but not all of it is important for later in **life**. What's important is to learn how to decide what's going to give us the **power** to **create** the **future** we want for ourselves and the world we live in.

CRUSHES & COMMITMENTS

Our friends Andy and Claudine hooked up in bio this year. It was one of those "love at first sight" things. It doesn't always happen that way, though. Someone you're crushing on may not even know you exist, or vice versa. Maybe you even have a long list of crushes. Or maybe your crush already has a girlfriend or boyfriend. Maybe your "relationship" only lasted a week . . . or even one date. Or maybe you're really good friends, like best friends, with someone, and you don't want to take the chance of complicating that friendship.

Whatever the case may be, we're basically just exploring our feelings and compatibility with other people we're attracted to. You've probably heard stories of "high school sweethearts" who got married and lived "happily ever after," but more often than not, the relationships we're in now won't last a lifetime. Of course, that doesn't mean the memories won't last, so try to make them the best they can be.

Sure, hookups happen in school all the time, but try not to make school all about that. Obviously, when it comes to school and dating, there will be drama. Even Andy and Claudine, the "love birds" who make us want to gag sometimes, have experienced it. When you're in the middle of some major drama at school, try not to lose focus on your classes and activities. The drama will pass, but missing schoolwork because of it may have lasting consequences on your grades. So, try not to get so caught up in the drama that you fall behind.

Are we talking about anyone we know?

INVOLVEMENT

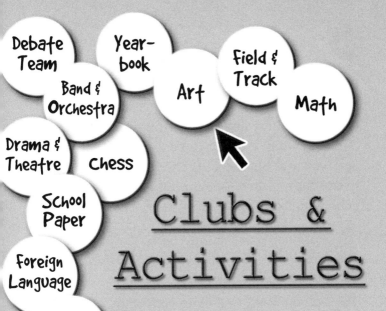

Debate Team

Year-book

Field & Track

Band & Orchestra

Art

Math

Drama & Theatre

Chess

School Paper

Clubs &
Activities

Foreign Language

Books

Gov't & Politics

You probably know of at least one person at your school who's like on every team and in **every** club. We call that **overkill**! In fact, that's the keyword. Great if they can keep it up, but *really*.

Football

Computers

Cheer-leading

Envi-ronment

Dance

It's not necessary to be a part of everything. For us, though, it's important to be **part** of something . . . something we like, something that **challenges** our **minds** and/or our **bodies**, something that puts us out there in the **world**. Participating in clubs and other activities is also a **good** way to find friends or at least acquaintances who have common **interests**.

53

Since we already have XTREMELY busy schedules with **homework**, studying, **socializing**, and **family** stuff, we need to **choose** carefully when deciding what we want to be a part of. Too much and we'll get burned out. There are lots of things to **consider** when figuring out what fits into your schedule, like:

- When does the club or activity meet?
- How often? How long does it last?
- Where does it take place?
- Do you need to devote weekends or evenings to it? How often?
- Does it require practice?
- Does it involve travel?
- Does it cost $$ (like do you have to buy instruments and/or equipment)?

All these points are **important** when you're trying to figure out which club or activity is for you.

What's more important is what your **interests** are. If you have a lot of interests, make a list and **rate** them from 1 to 10. Then check if the top-rated activities fit into your **schedule**.

Getting involved in something you like with **like-minded** people can help in lots of ways. You'll make new friends, learn stuff, and most of all, it looks good on your **college app**.

"Which Club or Activity Is for You" quiz on jonandjayne.com Check out the

Max's Story

The School Newspaper

When I was in elementary school, I started a class newspaper. It worked it out pretty well, considering I wrote it in pen, used copy paper, and drew squares for the different sections, some of which got shortened for artistic reasons (true fact: my entire sports section consisted of THE MARLINS HAD A GREAT HALFTIME SHOW WITH BILLY THE FISH). I gave up after a few issues, and then forgot about school newspaper—until middle school when my language arts teacher suggested we start one.

I wasn't a huge fan of my language arts teacher (for the last time, I didn't throw the stupid spitball), but I figured it would be fun, especially because I felt bad for not doing any school activities. So I showed up for the first meeting, along with some other people and one of my good friends. What I quickly found is this: writing newspapers is harder than you'd think. Let me give you a few examples:

1. Writing editorials is difficult when the "cartoonist" (only there for the Oreos) repeatedly tackles you from behind.

2. Pausing in the middle of a movie review to air-guitar the solos to AC/DC songs is generally frowned upon. (Especially when the particular solo involves you rocking out so hard that you rip out the cord to the computer next to you where someone else was writing—but not saving—an article.)

3. You have to actually have articles. Apparently, you're not allowed to just have three editorials, a cartoon, and two reviews.

4. Telling people who write to your advice column to "stop whining" is also generally frowned upon.

5. When you're doing a music review, you're not allowed to review Led Zeppelin and Rush albums from the 1970s. You have to review things other people listen to.

• READER SURVEY • JMHT

We care about your opinions! Take a minute to fill out HCI's online Reader Survey at http://survey.hcibooks.com, and you'll get a coupon toward future book purchases and a special gift available only online! Or you can mail this card back to us.

First Name _____ MI. _____ Last Name _____

Street Address _____ City _____ State _____ Zip _____

E-mail address _____

1. Are you . . .
□ Female? □ Male?

2. How old are you?
□ 8 or younger □ 9–12
□ 13–16 □ 17–20 □ 21+

3. Did you receive this book as a gift?
□ Yes □ No

4. Where do you usually buy books? (choose one)
□ Book Club/Mail Order
□ Bookstore
□ Internet
□ Price Club such as Costco
□ Retail Store such as Target

5. What type of magazine do you like best? (choose one)
□ Celebrity News
□ Fashion & Advice
□ Gaming
□ Music News

□ Sports
□ Religious

6. What type of book do you like best? (choose one)
□ Fiction
□ Self-Improvement
□ Reality/Memoir
□ Sports
□ Series books

7. What's your favorite website?

BUSINESS REPLY MAIL

FIRST-CLASS MAIL   PERMIT NO 45   DEERFIELD BEACH, FL

POSTAGE WILL BE PAID BY ADDRESSEE

The Jon & Jayne Doe Series
3201 SW 15th Street
Deerfield Beach FL 33442-9875

6. Sneaking into his articles and leaving funny messages will REALLY make the editor-in-chief mad. Especially if you're also an editor-in-chief and he can't fire you.

7. Nobody likes reading test tips,[*] and if you print them everyone will laugh at you, even if you explain that the language arts teacher made you.

So there. I will tell you this—school newspapers and extracurricular activities are usually fun. Just make sure not to rip out too many cords, and it will make your life a lot easier.

—Max V.

Seems like Max learned some good lessons during his stint as editor-in-chief. FUN is, of course, a big consideration when joining a club or sport. Why participate in something that bores you? Even something academic can be fun for some people. Fun is a *subjective* term. That means that everyone has their own opinion of what they think is fun. So find out for yourself what gets you excited and remember this keyword: **participate**.

[*]See, Jayne,
I told you so.

School with a Twist

Our school is as **traditional** as they come, and that's **okay** with us. You know, we have the standard 7 periods with a **lunch** break. Aside from some **electives**, our classes are all the basic **subjects**, like some version of math, English, science, social studies, phys-ed, and so on.

At some schools though, things aren't so traditional. We call that "**school with a twist**." These include **alternative** schools, religious schools, career and technical **education** schools, and **art-focus** schools.

Alternative schools are usually smaller than traditional schools, so the kids get more attention from their teachers—and from their classmates. In **religious** schools, religion plays a big part in

58

the studies with some classes and events that focus on religion. **Career** and **technical** education schools are places where the kids learn a trade that helps **prepare** them to work immediately after high school. (But **college** is still an option.) **Art-focus** schools are schools that may be available to kids who have an **xtraordinary** talent in the arts—like drama, dance, music, and drawing/painting.

It's really **cool** that schools like these are available, and that our **country** helps to prepare us for future **success** by making sure we all attend school. In some parts of the world, kids don't have the same **opportunities** as us. Some kids don't even go to school—either because there are **no schools** where they live or because they have to work to help **support** their families.

As much as school might be a pain and all the **responsibilities** might be a bit **overwhelming**, we really are very **fortunate** when it comes right down to it. Besides, what would we do all day without **school?***

*Surf, play video games, eat, sleep, shop, watch TV . . .

Ok, Jayne, I think we get the idea.

j/k JON.

Brittney's Story

Ballet Girl

It has always been my dream to be a professional ballerina. But it takes complete dedication and a lot of hard work to get there. The training is very intense, giving me quite a busy schedule. When you really want to make a career out of ballet, there's just no way you can go to a standard high school. A lot of girls who want to dance professionally wind up being home-schooled or take online high school courses. But luckily for me, there's a high school in the city that was designed to be flexible for high school students pursuing a profession in the arts or in sports.

It was perfect for me. But it was also very different

from my old high school. I had transferred from a parochial high school in the suburbs to a school in a big city. To name a few things, I no longer wear a uniform and I take the subway to school! (I didn't realize how spoiled I was to have a bus pick me up on my corner every morning!) The city is lots of fun, but in the winter it can be brutal to have to walk everywhere! As soon as I started going to my new school, I loved it because my teachers were great and the kids who went to the school were very interesting. I found so many more people with common interests. But not all my friends are dancers; I have friends who are classical musicians, actors/actresses, singers, models, and more!

Unfortunately, because of my ballet schedule, I don't have too much time to hang out with my friends after school. But from 8 AM 'til 12:30 PM I am surrounded by such incredible talent, and I get to experience high school at its best. I never dread going to school, and although I can be pretty exhausted from ballet, I try to enjoy every moment of it because I know that two years will go by fast.

The environment of the school is very relaxed. We can have drinks and food in the classrooms, and we're free to leave during the day. But some really cool aspects are that I am exempt from gym (since

I am very physical in ballet) and that I only have to take the core subjects like math and history. Some kids even leave in the middle of the day, train for their profession, and then come back later.

Because we are all busy working on our art form, the teachers accept homework late and guided study is an option. Guided study is when you teach yourself a subject when you have to be absent for more than 3 days for a professional reason, so you don't fall behind. By way of e-mail, the teachers are always in contact if you have questions. What's better than that? I get to pursue a dream in the arts while not compromising my education. Every day I know that I am getting closer and closer to achieving my goal.

—Brittney F.

Brittney's school sounds awesome! And it seems like she's found a way to continue her education while she works toward her dream.

Everybody's got a dream, but we don't all have to go to a special high school to follow it. Study, practice, determination, and follow-through are key ingredients in making our dreams come true, wherever we go to school.

Ellora's story

The Meditation Connection

Every student in the world knows that being in
school can be stressful and often unbearable.
However, it doesn't have to be that way. I go to
a very unique school called the Maharishi School
of the Age of Enlightenment. At my school we
practice a form of meditation called Transcendental
Meditation (TM for short). As a result, getting
through school is a breeze. A lot of TV news
channels visit and film our school, including
Nickelodeon. They voted us "cool school of
the month."

But what is TM you may ask? TM is a simple,
effortless technique of deep rest that releases

stress and allows the mind and body to act with their fullest potential. For me, TM feels like a mind bath. It helps to wash away my fatigue and gives me energy to complete the tasks of the day.

Sometimes it's hard to find time to do TM. When I don't meditate, I notice that I am filled with anxiety and it is hard to get through my day. It is harder to focus in school and retain the information my teachers are giving me.

We meditate together at the beginning, middle, and end of the day. The results of meditation are obvious in my school. There has never been a bully in my school. The atmosphere in the school is very peaceful and friendly. As a result, it is really easy to fit in and be accepted for you are. This, above all other things, is what has gotten me through school.

We are taught that when we meditate all of the different parts of our brain are enlivened. Connections are made between the different parts of the brain and increase total brain functioning. Many scientific studies have shown that this restful time will make us smarter, while we become more peaceful and content. This in turn boosts my academic performance. I am developing my brain! Isn't that cool?!

It may sound like we are all monks, but that is not true at all. I live a completely normal life. I go to parties, have lots of wonderful friends, play varsity sports, read fashion magazines, and watch lots of movies. What's different is that I have a technique to keep me grounded and alert. Anyone can learn to meditate no matter what religion, race, or background they have.

TM has made my school career easy and enjoyable and is one of the most rewarding things I do with my time. If everyone practiced TM, the entire world could be as peaceful as my school. Can you imagine that?

—Ellora H.

Ommmm. You've probably heard that sound, maybe even made it. But do you know what it means? After reading Ellora's story, we looked it up . . . *Om* is a mantra—a repeated word or phrase that helps concentration during meditation and similar activities. Om (pronounced *aaauuummm*, with 3 syllables) is believed by some to be the spoken essence of the universe. Hmmmm. Interesting stuff.

We bet you've got a **conundrum**—virtually all of us do. No, it's not a new deadly disease spread by infected purple-spined Chinese water dragons. It's a **problem**, usually w/ a **complex** answer.

If you've got a conundrum, go to jonandjayne.com and click on CONUNDRUMS & SOLUTIONS. We'll put our heads together and try to help you (and other people who have the same problem) with our "**solution**" in an upcoming issue.

We'll also check w/ **Dr. Toni** (see her bio on page 114) to be sure we're on the right track. Dr. Toni can be a bit **wordy**, but she's pretty **cool** and always has some good stuff to say.

But don't wait for us! If you've got a **serious** problem, talk to an **adult** you trust. Don't let your conundrum get the best of you. Find a **solution**!

Conundrums & Solutions

CONUNdrUM

My English teacher hates me! She gives me really bad grades no matter how hard I try. How am I supposed to make it through her class?

Jordan

SOLUtiON

She probably doesn't "hate" you, but it's possible she doesn't like something about you. Try to find out what the problem really is. Talk to her after class and let her know (in a polite way) that you are concerned about your grades and your "student/teacher" relationship (that takes guts, but do it anyway). If that doesn't help, you may want to talk to your guidance counselor and/or parents.

Dr. Toni Says:

When a student feels "hated" by a teacher, it's usually because there's something in the dynamic between them that is creating negative feelings. For example, the student may be struggling with the subject material and may show frustration as a result. This frustration may be unwittingly directed at the teacher or may be taken personally by him or her, causing the teacher to react negatively.

Yes, talking to the teacher is a good idea. If you are struggling, tell the teacher and set up a plan to get extra help. If it is not about your performance, talk about what you might be doing to irritate your teacher. Taking responsibility is important and part of the growing process. Of course, your teacher may be responsible for some of the negativity as well, and might simply need to be made aware that you are feeling disliked and unsupported.

■ ■ ■ ■ ■ ■

CONUNdrUM

Why does school have to be a social thing all the time? Why can't I just go there to learn and not have to worry about what I wear, who I sit with at lunch, and everything I say and do?

Keller

Solution

Some people are more affected by those around them than others. But, as with most stuff in life, we have to interact with other people. In school, we're learning how to deal with others one on one, in groups, with authority or peers, and so on. If you like to learn, look at interacting with people as a learning experience. Like it or not, we must have some social skills to go places in life. It's possible to get by without them, but it's not easy.

Dr. Toni Says:

Dealing with the social aspects of school is difficult for many people. Keller, you are not alone. You ask, "Why do I have to worry . . . ?" Well, you don't have to worry. As I say, "Every worry needs a plan." What that means is that it will be much more helpful to develop a plan to deal with your anxiety than to continue to worry unproductively.

Think about what you can do to make the situation better for yourself, to feel more comfortable, to feel accepted. What we say and do matters, so if you're having difficulty connecting with others, then some help with social skills is important. Learning to be friendly, assertive, and a good listener are just some of the components of social success. *Jon & Jayne's Guide to Making Friends and "Getting" the Guy (or Girl)* could be helpful with that.

Also, it is vital to learn to feel secure about yourself so that you do not take the words and actions of others personally. What we wear and how we present ourselves also matters. If you don't feel good about your appearance, do something to change it.

The reality is that school is not just a place for academics. It is also a place where we learn about people and relationships. So do look at it as a learning experience and make the best of it!

■ ■ ■ ■ ■ ■

CoNUNdrUM

There's this boy in my school who teases me, lies about me, and is so mean to me that it makes me think he doesn't want me to exist! What can I do?

Haina

SOLUtioN

Have you tried asking this boy straight out why he's so mean to you? If you decide to do that, try not to be all confrontational—just ask the question. Maybe he like "likes" you and doesn't know a better way to show it, or he's just trying to get your attention. (That doesn't make the way he's acting ok, though.) If you really feel threatened by him, we think you should speak to a school counselor or other trusted adult about it right away.

Dr. Toni Says:

The answer to this question may be complicated. Yes, it could be that the boy "likes" you and is trying to get your attention. Or it could be that he feels insecure and picks on you to feel more powerful and in control. Regardless of the reason, you do not deserve to be picked on and should do something about it right away.

Standing up to the boy will be important. Say to him in an assertive voice "Leave me alone!" It may be that he is picking on you because he perceives you as vulnerable or weak in some way. Let him know that you will not tolerate or put up with his teasing. Also, do tell a trusted adult—either a parent, teacher, or guidance counselor. They may need to work with the boy on controlling his behavior as well as improving his self-esteem so that he doesn't pick on others.

Harass This!

School **safety** is a BIG **issue**. We go to school to learn and **socialize**. The last thing we need is to feel **threatened** by another student. We've all heard about school shootings and that's really **scary**, but it's good to know events like those are pretty **rare**. What's not so rare, unfortunately, is **bullying** and **harassment**.

There are different types of bullying. A bully or a group of bullies may physically **threaten** classmates or **harass** them with verbal insults. Bullying can also include things like spreading **rumors**, pointing and **laughing**, name-calling, purposely bumping or knocking into someone, posting **nasty stuff** on the Internet, and going out of the way to **exclude** someone from something. Why do people act like that? It's hard to **figure** out.

Bullies are usually **insecure** people who take out their **fears** and frustrations on others. There's a good chance they've been bullied themselves—maybe even by a member of their **family**.

When bullies group together, or when they have followers, they can become **gang-like**. But sometimes bullies aren't that **obvious**. It could be the boy or girl on your bus who picks on you because you're **different** (from them). Or it could be a cold shoulder from a group you used to **hang out** with. Even someone who calls you names or makes up **rumors** about you is being a bully.

Whatever the case, bullies **harass** other people to make themselves feel like they are the ones in control. Don't give anyone control over your **self-respect**. If you firmly tell the bully to leave you alone, he or she just might do that.

"Never be bullied into silence. Never allow yourself to be made a victim. Accept no one's definition of your life; define yourself."

HARVEY FIERSTEIN, ACTOR & PLAYWRIGHT
WHO HAS A VERY GRAVELLY VOICE

Let's see what Dr. Toni has to say on the subject.

Dr. Toni's

BULLYING
Plain *and* Simple

Hey! As you know, bullying is a big problem. Dealing with bullies takes a lot of courage and requires active steps in stopping the behavior. Please don't stand by and let yourself or other kids get picked on. *You* can do something about it! *You* can help stop bullying! Both the victim and the bully need help. Read on . . .

Take this quiz. Check all that apply.

☐ I've called people names or teased them, talked or posted negative stuff online about somebody, been physically aggressive, or taken things from somebody at school.

☐ I feel kind of bad about myself, but don't know how to say it or what to do about it. Instead, I pick on others who seem weaker than me in some way.

☐ People don't like me unless I act tough. The only good thing about me is that I can control or have power over others.

If you checked ANY of these boxes, YOU ARE ACTING LIKE A BULLY, and you need to do something about it NOW.

not the Bully? Take this quiz.

☐ I've been called names or teased, have been pushed around, or have had things taken from me at school.

☐ I feel kind of bad about myself, but I don't know how to say it or what to do about it. I let myself get picked on by others who seem stronger or "cooler" than me in some way.

☐ People don't like me because I'm quiet, weak, or "different." I tend to be by myself a lot and stay under the radar.

If you checked ANY of these boxes, YOU MAY BE A VICTIM OF BULLYING, and you need to do something about it NOW.

Did you notice that bullies and victims are a lot alike? That's because both are suffering from poor **self-esteem.** One acts tough because of it and the other withdraws because of it. So, in either case, you must work to **feel better** about yourself by changing your **thinking** and your **behavior.**

Here's what you can do about it:

If you're the BULLY, take these steps:

1 Take a DEEP BREATH and say, *"I can change my behavior. I'm a good person doing bad stuff."*

2 Talk to your guidance counselor, parent, aunt, uncle, or other trusted adult. Tell them that you are bullying people and that you want to stop.

3 Work with a counselor of some sort to come up with a PLAN for stopping your behavior.

4 Your PLAN should involve REDEFINING yourself as someone who is cool, athletic, smart, or some other great quality that you have, but may not even know yet. You need to discover what your GREAT quality is and OWN IT. When you feel better about yourself, you will stop picking on other people.

If you're the VICTIM, take these steps:

1 Take a DEEP BREATH and say, *"I won't let people walk all over me anymore. I will stand up for myself!"*

2 Talk to your guidance counselor, parent, aunt, uncle, or other trusted adult. Tell them that you are being bullied and want help.

3 Work with a counselor of some sort to come up with a PLAN for being more ASSERTIVE and STICKING UP FOR YOURSELF.

4 Your PLAN should involve REDEFINING yourself as someone who is cool, athletic, smart, or some other great quality that you have, but may not even know it yet. You need to discover what your GREAT quality is and OWN IT. When you feel better about yourself, you will stop letting others pick on you.

Work to understand your thinking. What are your actions telling you about yourself? In the table below are some examples of self-defeating (negative) thoughts and how you can change them to be more self-affirming (positive). Work with someone who can help you to CHALLENGE the negative thoughts and see how they really DON'T MAKE SENSE. By practicing saying these new things, you can improve your SELF-ESTEEM.

Self-Defeating	Self-Affirming
No one likes me.	X, Y, and Z like me.
I'm just not good at anything.	I'm good at X, Y, and Z.
My parents get mad at me, so I must be an idiot. I bet they don't really love me.	My parents get mad at my behavior, but they still love me. Sometimes they're just angry and it's not even about me.
I'm a loser.	I'm a good person.
I have no friends.	When I'm friendlier, kinder, and more outgoing, I'll make friends.
I don't like how I look.	I can take better care of myself so I look my best.

It's not easy, but if you take SMALL STEPS to change your thoughts and your behavior, you can change your life and be happier. If you're happier, you'll be less likely to be a BULLY . . . or a VICTIM.

www.cyberbullies.uck

Bullies and people who get bullied have been around for like forever. Our parents and grandparents probably have some stories to share about who did what to who—and it will probably sound a lot like what goes on today . . . with one big exception: the Internet. (BTW, how did they live without being connected?!). Technology, as great as it is, also has a dark side and cyberbullying is part of it.

What is it exactly? It's sending hurtful and/or threatening messages via IM, email, or text. It's posting hurtful and/or threatening messages on websites. It's also posting some-one's personal info (like messages, videos, and/or photos) on websites or sending them to other users.

It's difficult to combat cyberbullying because in many cases the bullies don't identify themselves. If you are being cyberbullied, chances are you know who it is, though. But it may be hard to prove. And even if you can prove it, what can be done about it? It's a CONUNDRUM alright.

There are websites out there that give advice and sug-gestions on what to do about this abuse. And it IS abuse. Don't let youself be bullied—even electronically. Do some research to find out how to stand up for yourself online.

John's

t o r y

Bullies & Violence

Violence and bullies go together because without bullies, there wouldn't be as much violence. You are destined to find bullies in any school you go to, no matter where.*

Bullies tend to be "bullies" only when others are around. Their problem is that they try to seem cool and get attention any way they can, and sometimes that means hurting others. If you were in a room alone, with just the bully and you, he or she would probably be a lot nicer. Bullies are usually insecure, and sometimes they are in the most pain of all. Usually, their families don't seem to care

*John, read Ellora's story on page 63.

about them or have no time for them. Maybe their parents are divorced or a death has happened in the family. Maybe they have no friends, or they used to get bullied when they were little. It seems like no one really knows or understands.

Sure, bullying others isn't the best way to solve problems, but hating them and being mean back isn't much better. Maybe you could try talking to them or at least being nice to them. If you don't want to do that, just leave them alone. Don't bother them, and maybe they won't bother you.

Violence is never the answer, no matter what. A lot of people think being mean and hurtful to others is cool and think that being "bad" is the cool thing. I'll bet if bullies tried being more respectful, then they would like it much better than acting cold-hearted and cruel.

Basically, the point is, being a bully isn't all that . . . "cool." Choosing that kind of lifestyle just gives you a bad rep and shows that you're scared and in need of any kind of attention.

—John "Mikey" Y.

Mikey's got some good insight into the whole bullying thing. We're all just trying to figure out what makes some people tick.

A LESSON FROM GREAT-GRANDPA K

I WAS A KID DURING THE WAR. MOST FAMILIES WERE STRUGGLING, BUT I FELT LIKE EVERYONE HAD MORE THAN MINE. THIS MADE ME FEEL REALLY BAD ABOUT MYSELF.

BACK WHEN I WENT TO SCHOOL, WE HAD TO USE OUR FEET TO GET THERE. I WALKED TEN CITY BLOCKS TO SCHOOL AND BACK HOME AGAIN. WE ALSO HAD TO WALK BACK AND FORTH FOR LUNCH. RAIN, SNOW, WIND, COLD, HEAT—SURE ENOUGH, I WALKED THROUGH IT ALL. THE SOLES OF MY SHOES WERE SO WORN THAT I HAD TO PUT CARDBOARD IN THEM.

I DIDN'T REALLY LIKE SCHOOL, BUT I WENT BECAUSE THAT IS WHAT WE HAD TO DO. I WORE THE SAME CLOTHES ALL THE TIME. ONE DAY, WHEN I FINALLY WORE SOMETHING NEW, MY TEACHER MADE ME STAND UP IN FRONT OF THE CLASS. MAYBE SHE THOUGHT SHE WAS BEING NICE, BUT IT ONLY MADE ME FEEL WORSE.

I picked fights a lot because I thought I was one of the toughest kids going. Since I had so little, being tough made me feel important.

One day a boy from another country joined our class. I was bullying him outside school, and he punched me in the mouth and knocked my front tooth loose. He also knocked some sense into me, and I didn't hit him back.

I had never backed down from a fight before, but I suddenly felt sorry for this boy. He had no friends and couldn't speak our language. He had even less than me, but he still stood up for himself.

A few days later part of my front tooth turned black. (It was a long time before I had my tooth replaced, so I lived with that reminder for many years.)

Something clicked in me that day, and I stopped picking fights. And you know what? I felt better about myself. Eventually I became a grownup, like most people do, but I'll never forget that kid or how my life changed after he stood up to me.

OH, BEHAVE!

Every school has a **discipline code**. What you can or can't get away with at one school may be very different at another school. The reason for the codes are to keep us **safe** and to make sure the school environment is one that we can **learn** in. We may not like all the **rules**—we don't have to—but we know it's best to follow them to avoid **detention** or, worse, **suspension**.

The **obvious** things that can land someone in the **principal's** or **dean's** office are drug or alcohol use, drug pushing or dealing, **smoking** cigarettes, **fighting**, skipping classes, and **cheating**. Being outright rude to teachers or other school authorities will probably get you detention (or suspension), too. Obviously, all of those things are really bad ideas, especially if you want to stay out of **trouble**.

The policies on using **cell phones** are different for different schools. In our school, we aren't allowed to use our cell phones during class. They have to be **turned off** and out of sight. In some schools, though, there are kids who actually **text** or play **games** during class. That's just not happening where we go.

Who dishes out the **discipline** might be the principal, an AP, or a dean. They might seem a little **intimidating**, but remember, they're people too. If you get yourself into trouble, be **straight** with them. Having an **attitude** is just going to make the situation worse.

Are you always getting in **trouble**? Maybe you're looking for some **attention**. Think about that.

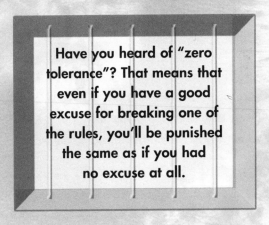

Have you heard of "zero tolerance"? That means that even if you have a good excuse for breaking one of the rules, you'll be punished the same as if you had no excuse at all.

Chandra's

Story

Dealing with the Dean

Mr. Barry S. is the best dean. He may be strict, but that's only because he knows what's good for his students . . . and what isn't. When I arrive at school, Mr. S is always there to greet me and the other students with a big smile. He treats us like we are his own kids. He watches out for us, jokes around with us, and even defends us when we get in trouble for something he knows we didn't do. I know I can talk to Mr. S about anything, and he'd help me with any problem I need to solve.

For me, a trip to Mr. S's office is not rare. That doesn't mean I always get into trouble—it simply means that I pop into his office every day to say hi or help him with his filing or paperwork or to pick up stuff for teachers.

Even though Mr. S has an important job, he knows how to have fun. The other day, I was his monitor along with my friend Cynthia. While we were hanging out, we started to sing. Mr. S, busy typing away, looked up from his keyboard and said, "Chandra, who sings that song?"

"Danity Kane," I responded. "Good, let's keep it that way," he replied. In his very next breath, he asked me what I did with the money. "Money, what money?" I asked. "The money your parents gave you for singing lessons," he said with a smile.

Sometimes Mr. S is all business, but I don't blame him for paying more attention to his work than to us. He has a lot of responsibility.

This year, I will be going on to high school. The number-one thing that I think most students are going to miss when we leave middle school is Mr. S (especially me). The new kids coming to middle school next year are really lucky that they'll have him to turn to for advice or help. I hope there will be somebody like him at my high school who I can build that special bond with.

—Chandra P.

"AARON DETENTION"

Chandra's right: Mr. S is really cool (when he wants to be). He's also funny (when he wants to be). He reminds me of Stone Cold Steve Austin. (I guess it's a wrestling thing, because he's also a HS wrestling ref.) I know I'm not one of the best students, but he still finds a way to set me straight. If he's in a so-so mood, he'll only give me five days lunch detention. But when he's in a bad mood, he's like, "Two weeks!"

I don't mean any disrespect to him, and sometimes I say things I shouldn't. For example, right now, I'm serving a five-day in-school suspension for calling him by his first name, Barry. (I shouldn't have done that and won't do it again for two reasons: one is that I know I should respect my elders, and two, I don't want to get in trouble again.) Still, I think Barry (just kidding) is mad cool, and he's always cracking jokes. He calls me "Aaron Detention"—I guess because I get it a lot.

My advice is "Don't tick off the dean." Mr. S is cool until you mess with him. If you screw up, you pay. There are no second chances. It's probably that way with a lot of other deans too. Mr. S is a good dean, but better yet, he is a great man.

—Aaron G.

After-school Recovery

Winding down after a day of school can mean lots of things to different people. Here are some ways you can recharge yourself, the same way you'd recharge your iPod or phone:

- Get together with **friends**
- Listen to or play **music**
- Talk on the **phone**
- Play a video or computer **game**
- Write in your journal or on your **blog**
- Watch a good TV **show**
- Read a **book**
- Have a **snack**
- Take a short **nap**
- **Exercise**
- Visit your MySpace page or **jonandjayne.com**
- Eat **french fries**

French fries? Who knows? There are lots of different ways to wind down after a long **grueling** day at **school**. But what if there's no time? It's true: Some days we may not even get a chance to recharge. Stuff like tons of **homework**, studying for a big **test**, after-school activities, **babysitting** for younger siblings, helping with **dinner**, and other things get in the way. Yeah, these are things we **have to do**, but we also need to remember that it's important to take time for **ourselves** and just **chill**—for a little while at least.

If you find yourself **overextended**, think about what you can do to ease the pressure. Some people love all the **activity**, and that's great. But if you **think** there's too much on your **schedule** and you don't have a chance to just **be yourself** for a little while every day and that bothers you, make a **list** of your responsibilities, **priorities**, and activities. Figure out how much time each thing takes and how much **time** you have. Bet you'll discover that you actually do have some time to **squeeze** in for yourself.

Ian's story

My Guitar Gets Me Through the Day

Every school day is the same, yet different in its own way, just like us as people. While it appears different due to different events or obstacles, it's really just like every other day. Even though it is almost exactly like the days preceding it, today or tomorrow can seem a lot harder than it really is because we tend to overdramatize all the little things that change in our day. But also, we have to adapt to our environment in order to survive . . . or at least to enjoy life. With me, personally, I get through the day using my key to happiness: my guitar.

When I play my guitar, it's just an ultimate release of my stress, tension, and anger. It's sort of like a portal that allows me to let loose and see things in perspective. It's a truly amazing feeling that makes me who I am, helps me shape who I want to be, and figure out what I want to do with my life.

Before I played the guitar, I was miserable and depressed. I would wake up every morning wishing that I could relive yesterday, but, of course, yesterday left and was gone forever, and because of spite, I hated today because it had taken yesterday away from me, just like tomorrow would do to today. It's sort of confusing, but it made sense to me.

Well, after a while of this endless cycle, I tried to do something to occupy my time, so I began to take guitar lessons. After about a month, I had fallen in love with this instrument. Day after day, week after week, I practiced each day, getting a little better. My endless cycle began to change into a daily condition of satisfaction, and the pain I had faced every day had been lifted, letting me live my life, instead of regretting it. So, in a way, my guitar had become a kind of therapy that let me look at my life in perspective and see that I had it too good to be so pessimistic.

Now I'm not saying that the answer to getting through the school day is playing guitar. Maybe instead of playing music, listening to music is your escape, or maybe it has nothing to do with music at all. It could be running, shopping, or just talking to someone you trust. Whatever it is, the answer is out there, waiting for you find it, or just waiting for you to recognize that it's been there your whole life trying to get you to realize your life is better than it seems or is going to get better in time.

Remember, the way you get through the day doesn't matter, but the fact that you *can* make it means everything.

—Ian B.

Ian's an amazing guitarist—he even spent part of the summer at guitar camp. It's great that he found something he loves to help him unwind.

Music is one option, but there are lots of others. There's a good chance you can also find something to help you feel good about yourself. We think it makes getting through all the other stuff we HAVE to do a little easier.

Michael's story

I Like School

I actually like going to school. I've been going there most of my life, all my friends go there, and the teachers know me. I'm also a pretty good student. I do well in almost every subject.

I usually go to bed early on school nights so I'm well rested. I take a shower at night because in the morning I don't have enough time.

At lunch, I mostly play basketball with my friends. One of the things that all my friends have in common is that we love playing sports like basketball, baseball, and football. Knowing that I have something I really like to do at lunch makes getting through the morning easier.

Depending on the season, I play different sports after school. And that helps me get through the afternoons. In spring and fall I play baseball, and in winter I play in basketball. Some of my friends play too, but we're not always on the same team. It used to bother me, but now I enjoy meeting new people and having different teammates.

My teachers don't give us tons of homework, so I like to get it done right when I get home. That way I have time for myself. I like to hang out at the high school, a couple of blocks away. My friends and I might just shoot hoops or hang out and talk. I also like to watch high school sports.

By hanging out with friends, playing sports, and doing well in school, I get through the day okay, maybe even better than some other kids.

—Michael S.

Michael sounds pretty well rounded, and he's got a positive outlook. Sports keep him involved with other people who share his interests, and they really seem to help him get through the day—not that it sounds like he needs much help! If he didn't have sports and friends, though, he might not find school so likeable.

Crushin' on a Teacher?

Do you have a "thing" for your teacher? We've heard it's pretty normal. Likeable and attractive teachers will most likely have more than one student crushing on him or her, so you're not alone. Keep your crush in perspective though. A trusted teacher will NEVER act on inappropriate feelings with an underage student. Doing so is abnormal, not to mention illegal.

To help deal with your crush, it's good to keep in mind that your teacher has a life outside of school that may even include a husband or wife and children. It also helps to know that crushes on teachers usually don't last for very long. Sure, it's fun to daydream occasionally, but if you find that you can't think about anything else, talk about your feelings with a trusted adult. It's not a good idea to share your feelings with your teacher, though. It will just result in major awkwardness.

Use your crush to your advantage: figure out what qualities it is you like about your teacher. Then find someone your own age who has those or similar qualities. Then make a connection with that person and let your crush on your teacher fade away.

BEEN THERE DONE THAT

S chool can be a **tough** place no matter who you are. Whether you're the cute cheerleader, **popular** jock, or band **geek**, the gossiping hallways and threatening classrooms don't **discriminate**. It doesn't have to be so tough though! Check out the **advice** of some college students our friend Stephanie interviewed who have been through it, because they know exactly what middle school and high school can be like.

Josh D., 19: Middle and high school is all about free expression, and it's really the only time where you can be (almost) completely uninhibited. I wish I would have been more true to myself. I feel that being open about the kind of person I am would have made getting through school a lot simpler for me.

Alexandra J., 18: I wish I had tried harder in school and gotten higher grades. A lot of your study habits in college come from what you did in high school. I also still kick myself for not getting to know some people better. I should have taken more time to learn more about people who I never really got to know that well.

Harley S., 19: I would have become physically active sooner. I was really out of shape until I went on a diet my junior year of high school. Five months later I was 70 pounds lighter and much healthier. Losing the weight helped me be more social, and I found myself enjoying school more. Overall, I would have started taking better care of myself sooner because it really altered my outlook on school.

Michelle D., 23: I would have to say that all the high school drama really isn't that important when you look back on it. The situations that you thought were the end of the world as you knew it really were not that big of a deal. Just remember even the hottest, cutest, most athletic, smartest kid in school falls in the snow in the parking lot of high school. Everyone is human and has embarrassing moments too, and people eventually forget them.

Jim C., 20: Balance out school work and your social life. Both are important, and at the end of the day, if you focus on one too much then you're going to miss out. Take time to do both, and you will have made the most of your adolescent years.

Mike F., 19: If there is any one thing I could go back and change, it's to not procrastinate as much as I did. I put off all my work and studying until the very last minute and all it did was stress me out. Once I hit college, I had to work hard to break a habit that I shouldn't have made in the first place. If I had learned to work at a steady pace instead of procrastinating, I probably would have had ended up with more free time.

Dana J., 19: If I were to change anything about my high school experience, I would have been friends with all different groups of people instead of just sticking to my small group of friends. I also wish I wasn't so shy because now that I'm not, I'm so much happier and a lot more social.

Sara S., 21: The main thing I would change would be to have gone to school more than I did. I thought it was cool to skip school and hang out with my friends, but I really wish I had learned more in high school. I would have also joined more clubs to beef up my college application because those extra activities really do matter.

Josh P., 18: As distracting as cute girls can be, I regret letting one get in between me and my best friend. I stole a girl from him and ruined our friendship for a relationship that didn't last very long anyway. In the end, it's your friends who are most important, and I wish I didn't have to learn it the hard way.

Stephanie D., 20: Get involved in something you like right from the start! I waited until my junior year of high school to get involved with the yearbook club. Those first two years weren't great for me because a lot of my old friends chose the wrong path. But as soon as I joined the yearbook crew, I found some amazing friends. It was the best decision I made in high school. . . . I just wish I had done it sooner.

Gotta love a **quiz!** This issue's **Quickie** has 10 mostly **school-related** Qs from Quiz-Master Anthony P. See if you know the answers. If not, **Google** it. Then go to **jonandjayne.com** to see if you're right. Click on "**QUICKIES**." The password is **KNOWLEDGE**. Catch the "Fresh Factoids" for each answer.

#1 In Stephenie Meyer's TWILIGHT book series, what high-school grade is Bella Swan in when she first comes to Forks, Washington?

#2 What does the acronym S.A.T. stand for?

#3 Who ran for the position of class president in NAPOLEON DYNAMITE?

#4 If you're a sophomore, how many years do you have left before you graduate high school?

#5 In the movie MEAN GIRLS, what was the name of the clique that tormented Lindsay Lohan's character at school?

#6 What's the name of the wizard school that Harry Potter attends?

#7 What happens to sixteen-year-old Juno MacGuff (Ellen Page) in JUNO?

#8 What's attached to the string that sits atop a high school graduation cap?

#9 What's the name of the East High basketball team in HIGH SCHOOL MUSICAL?

#10 The women's basketball team that radio DJ Don Imus "dissed" on the radio in 2007 played for which college?

VENT

When it comes to what we **want** from school and what our **parents** want for us, there's going to be a difference in **priorities**. Some parents think that nothing's more important than getting good **grades**, others might think it's joining lots of clubs, and some parents just want their kids to stay out of **trouble**.

In some cases, there are parents who might not seem to **care** what goes on at school at all. And then you've got the complete **opposite** of that—the parents who are online all the time checking up on the daily **reports** from the school.

Leesa says:

"My mother is constantly checking Edline so she can remind me to study for upcoming tests —and I'm not allowed to have study partners. She doesn't have to be like that! I'm a really good student! I have like NO privacy!"

SECRET: Leesa has a history test tomorrow, but she also made plans to see her boyfriend, Jeff. When her mom drops her off at the library after school, she's meeting Jeff there—maybe they'll study, maybe they won't.

Darren says:

66My parents are really busy with high-pressure jobs and everything. Sometimes I think they don't even care about how I do in school.99

SECRET: Darren is going to purposely fail the history test tomorrow to see if his parents notice.

Leo says:

66My parents won't let me quit band. I've been in band for years, but I don't like it anymore. I'm more into hanging out with my friends.99

SECRET: Leo is going to skip band practice (again) to hang out with his friends.

Shaina says:

66My dad thinks I should get a solo at the concert just because my mom had a great voice when she was alive. I know I'm not as good as she was, and I'm not going to get the solo.99

SECRET: Shaina's father is going to call the chorus director and push for her to get the solo.

When it comes to **school**, do you know what your parents expect from you? Do you know what you **expect** from yourself—and from your parents? Those are some good **questions**. See if you can figure out if you're on the same **page** as your parents. If not, maybe you can come to some sort of **compromise** with them or at least talk about what's on your mind.

Let's see how things worked out for Leesa, Darren, Leo, and Shaina:

RESULT: Leesa and Jeff met at the library. Jeff quizzed her on the history questions, and she knew most of the answers. So they left to get something at Starbucks, but Leesa's mom was there getting coffee. There was a big shouting match, and Leesa was grounded. She was so upset she did poorly on the history exam. Her mom blamed it on her "date," but Leesa insisted she was bummed about the fight and couldn't concentrate. They never resolved the issue.

RESULT: Darren did poorly on the history test too. In fact, he failed it just like he planned. When his teacher finally reached his parents, they talked to Darren about it, and he told them that if they didn't care when he got good grades, why should they care if he got bad ones? That was the first step in getting them to realize they weren't paying enough attention, and they decided to make some changes. (Darren wasn't entirely happy about it, though, because now it seemed like they were too much into his business. Sometimes, you just can't win.)

RESULT: Leo skipped one too many band practices and got himself kicked out. His parents were really upset, and he was angry with them for not letting him just quit. They didn't speak for a few days, but finally, they all agreed that Leo would continue to practice with a private instructor. Leo was okay with that, since it was only one hour a week. He told his parents he'd consider rejoining band next year.

RESULT: Well, Shaina got the solo, but she knew she wasn't the best one in chorus. She told her dad how uncomfortable she was that she'd been chosen and could not figure out why. Her dad came clean with what he'd done. Shaina spoke to the director about it, and he decided there would be two solos this year. When Shaina did her solo, she was better than she thought she'd be.

When it comes to **parents**, they usually have the final say. If you can't reason with them or get them to understand your **point of view**, it sometimes helps to just **vent** about it to friends or on paper . . . and then do what you have to do.

JaynE SaYs 611: I don't want to go to school tomoro

JD GaTEr 92:　　how come

JaynE SaYs 611: cause it's the last day

JD GaTEr 92:　　u should be celebrating

JaynE SaYs 611: Yeah. I'm just gonna miss it

JD GaTEr 92:　　itll be time to go back before u know it then u will say u dont want to go back

JaynE SaYs 611: it's a love-hate relationship

JD GaTEr 92:　　like ours?

JaynE SaYs 611: uh, u LOVE me?

JD GaTEr 92:　　figure of speech

JaynE SaYs 611: hmmm ok

JD GaTEr 92:　　I cant believe u r leaving for the whole summer

JaynE SaYs 611: i promise to send a postcard

JD GaTEr 92:　　Ya, we'll see. nite, jayne

JaynE SaYs 611: g'nite Jon ... I WILL miss u

JD GaTEr 92 has signed off.

School's Out!

Whew! Looks like we made it through another "issue." And **school** is one of the biggest issues, that's for sure.

We made some lasting **memories** and acquired some important knowledge that'll help us next year. And who knows, it just might come in handy when we're **adults**. Whether or not the memories are good is mostly up to us. Hopefully, you had some great times with good **friends** and cool **teachers**.

It's true that not everything at school is going to be **great**. When the year's over, we try to focus on the good things and, yeah, **learn** from the things that didn't go the way we wanted them to.

The **good news** is, every new school year we get a chance at a **fresh start**. Of course, you can have a fresh start anytime you set your **mind** to it —even if it's still the middle of the year.

Hey JON, A u going TO SUMMER school?

Why, Jayne, u looking for some company?

*What's the one thing you would wanna
tell the whole world if you could?*

We asked, and you answered.
Here's what some of you had to say. ⟶

Get heard, too. Go to jonandjayne.com
and click on "Tell the World!"
Then enter what you have to say.

Look for your message to the world
in an upcoming issue.

Tell the World

Stop fighting. It's killing our world.
············· Melina

In the end everything will be okay; if it's not okay, it's not the end.
Carla

Sammy · Life has many choices like a bowl of Skittles. You never know which to choose.

A big shot is just a little shot that keeps on shooting.
Skylar

Don't drown in your own spit.
Jeremy

live.life.love.
Hosana

Help us save the world and make it a better place.
Chandra

············· Screw that!
Asif

It's still all about the hair.
Ryan

Everything happens for a reason.
Ashley

Come to my house & peace out.
············· Melinda

Shopping is a sport too, ya know.
Melody

I love you.
Steven

Be respectful and care for one another.
Gabriela

Test everything.

Hello. Jim
Brian ············· Make peace.
Sofia

Stop the killings, fights, and stealing. Let's all just live in peace.
Lahaina

············· I don't know.
Sami

Help the people in need.
Danielle

Be the ball.
Garrett

The bad guys may get the cool lines and clothes, but look how often they actually win . . . never.
Wheeler

Appreciate everything you have around you.
············· Andrea

What doesn't kill you the first time usually gets rid of you in the second attempt so live life to the fullest.
Paolo

Peace, love, and rock & roll!
Allie

109

No Internet?!

That's OK. You can still be part of our **7F community**. To get the answers to the Quickie and the Drama, simply send a postcard to our publisher's place:

HCI Teens
3201 SW 15th Street
Deerfield Beach, FL 33442

Attention: Quickie & Drama Answers

CYA!

Thanks for hanging w/ us!
We hope you had fun and got something
out of our rantings and ramblings.
Hope you liked the stories from our
friends. Got a story of your own?
We'd really like to hear from you,
so don't forget to visit us at
www.jonandjayne.com.
There's more to do & more to come.
Join our 7F community and get heard!

~Jon & Jayne

School's out for summer . . .

"Don't cry because it's over.
Smile because it happened."
—Theodor Seuss Geisel (better known as Dr. Seuss)

Meet the #3 Crew

Hello, we're **Carol** and **Gary R.**, and we make it possible for Jon and Jayne to get their word out. We live in mostly sunny Florida with our two dogs, one cat, one parrot, one iguana—and our son, **Justin**, who introduced us to Jon and Jayne.

What's good? I'm **Aaron G.**, and I'm interested in a lot of things—sports mostly and video games. I have a girl-friend who's really beautiful and cool. My future goal is to be a forensics person or a lawyer.

I'm **Allie M.** and I'm a middle school student. I have a few interests: one is karate (in which I recently got my black belt) and the other is softball (I play first base and catcher). I love cooking and animals.

I'm **Ashley B.** I'm really into theater—I was student director of one of my high school shows. I dance a lot; it's my favorite hobby. I also enjoy hanging out with my friends. I'm in the sports medicine academy, and I want to be a doctor when I'm older.

My name is **Brittney F.** I'm a senior in high school in New York. I am training at a top ballet school to become a professional ballet dancer. I train for five hours a day. My other interests include reading, writing, and photography.

I'm **Carla C.** I'm a sophomore in high school. I like writing poetry, listening to music, and drinking Starbucks. I'm very shy with people I don't know. I want to be a photographer. I'm good at math, but I hate it.

I'm **Chandra P.** I'm 13 years old and attending school in NY. I love to go shopping and spend time with friends and family. I also love to listen to music and sing. I hope to become successful in the business world and even have a business with my family.

My name is **Ellora H.** and I live in Iowa. I am a senior at Maharishi School. I play sports, knit, draw, paint, take photos, play piano, read, act in plays, make jewelry, travel, and write. I believe that the purpose of life is finding happiness in everything you do.

 Hi, I'm **Dr. Toni**. I'm a licensed psychologist practicing in New York, and I've worked directly with kids and teens since 1999 in community and school settings. My specialty is running groups for preteen and teenage girls. I currently have a private practice in New York.

Hi, my name is **Ian B.** I am 15 years old, and I'm an aspiring musician. I work as a busboy in an Italian restaurant, and I'm the vice president of my school's creative writing club. I love my life, and I value every moment I have of being alive.

I'm **Jacob C.** I recently left my very large high school in Massachusetts to live with my dad and stepmom on Cape Cod and attend a very small high school nearby. I'll let you know what I think of the change! In the meantime, I'm a musician (with a recent interest in bluegrass), read voraciously, get around on a long board, and like going to concerts.

Hi, my name is **John Y.**, but people call me **Mikey**. I am 14 years old. I'm on the soccer team. My best friends are Ashley, Amanda, and Cole. I go online a lot, and I am always with my friends. I love to talk. I can't imagine being without music. My second home is the movie theater.

Hey it's me, **Justin O.** I am about 5'10", and I love sports and being active. I'm a sophomore in high school with a 3.3 grade point average. I also enjoy practicing karate. I have a junior black belt and an adult brown belt. Besides karate I also play football and basketball. All around, I'm a particularly athletic kid.

Hi, I'm **Kaitlyn R.** I'm 16. I love shopping, hanging out with my friends, and listening to music. I hate doing nothing. I think global warming is scary; something has to be done about it. The things about school I dislike the most are homework and tests! They're so annoying.

Hello. I'm **Matthew B.**, and I'm a high school English teacher in Florida. Long story short: I migrated south from Wisconsin four years ago and I am still thawing out. I love alligators, foreign languages, palm trees, and peel n' eat shrimp. Writing is my favorite hobby. Someday I'll live in Crete, in love, in peace, and in harmony with life.

Hey, my name is **Max V.**, and I belong to the holy church of chilling. I play video games, listen to music, hang out with my friends, and play guitar. I believe that rock heals all wounds.

My name is **Michael S.** I live in California, and I'm in junior high. I spend my free time playing baseball and basketball. I also like texting my friends, riding my bike, and swimming. My favorite food is pizza. I like to collect things like baseball cards, t-shirts, and hats.

Hey, I'm **Ryan ("Chili") P.**, and I'm 15. I'm a black belt in American Kenpo, and I really enjoy teaching the younger kids. I used to skateboard, but now I mostly play guitar (I taught myself). I also love to go to the beach and surf. One of my favorite things to do is listen to music. My favorite band is Led Zeppelin.

I'm **Samantha S.** I'm 15. I like music, movies, friends, and books. I talk to friends on MySpace a lot. One of my favorite movies is *The Princess Bride* and one of my favorite books is *Harry Potter and the Prisoner of Azkaban.* My friends make me laugh, but sometimes they do really stupid things. I dislike mean people.

Hi, my name is **Sammy M.** and I live in Florida. I'm 14 years old and in the 8th grade. I have two great dogs, Max and Justice. I'm a brown belt in karate, and I also run track at school. I like to hang out with my friends and go to movies.

Hi, my name is **Shivani P.** I live in Florida, and I'm in 8th grade. I love to talk and hang out with my friends. I like listening to music and I'm a huge JB fan. I also love meeting new people and making new friends. :P

My name is **Skylar H.** and I'm the teen crew captain. My friends are an extremely important part of my life, and so is my family. I love to make people laugh. I enjoy watching teen drama movies about relationships and reading books about the same kind of stuff. A big hobby of mine is working with children and making a difference in someone's life.

I'm **Wheeler B.**, and my three favorite things in general are karate, writing, and video games. My least favorite things are math and Brussels sprouts. Hey, just because I write essays doesn't mean I'm not normal. I get pretty good grades, and I have a black belt in MMA.

Hi. This is **QuizMaster Anthony P**. I love movies and music and books and art and TV (especially Ernie Kovacs—look him up online!). I have worked in book publishing my entire career, including three years in children's books. I'm a happy stepdad to twin teens, which keeps life interesting.

Where Can I Find...?

NORTH CAROLINA

DEAR JON,

HEY, HOW'S IT GOING? WEEK ONE OF TEEN TRAVEL WAS SO MUCH FUN. I'M MAKING LOTS OF NEW FRIENDS AND SEEING SOME REALLY COOL THINGS, BUT I MISS YOU SOOO MUCH! WE'LL BE LEAVING NC SOON AND HEADING FOR CHARLESTON, SC.

BTW, I MET THIS GUY ON THE TOUR WHO REMINDS ME OF YOU, AND I THINK HE LIKES ME! CYA SOON,

♡ JAYNE

P.S. I SAW A HUGE BLACK BEAR IN PERSON! BYE!

POSTMARK:
NORTH CAROLINA
JUL 2
9:30AM
2009
LOCAL BRANCH

JON DOE
123 FOURTH WAY
FRIENDSHIP, FL 33333

POSTCARD

Outbox
Outgoing

Andy CODE RED....
jayne met a guy on
the trip.....what am
I going to do...

SEND   BACK

Inbox
Incoming

Jon, man, when r u
just going to tell her
...hey maybe it will be
a quick summer fling...

DELETE   BACK